THE UK NINJA FOODI COOKBOOK 2023 SMARTLID

★★★★★

By: Judi Clark

TABLE OF CONTENTS
BREAKFAST

01 CHERRIES OATS

02 MUSHROOM AND SPINACH BAKE

03 ALMOND EGGS

04 SMOKED SAUSAGE BREAKFAST MIX

05 CREAM CHEESE AND BREAD BOWLS

06 YOGURT HASH BROWNS

FISH & SEAFOOD

07 SEA BASS FILLETS

08 ROSEMARY SHRIMP

09 TUNA AND SPINACH

10 PARMESAN SHRIMP

11 SALMON AND SPRING ONIONS

12 MISO SALMON

POULTRY

13 CHICKEN AND ONION SAUCE

14 CHICKEN MEATBALLS

15 PAPRIKA TURKEY

16 DUCK AND LENTILS

17 CHICKEN AND COURGETTE

18 CHICKEN AND CHILIES SAUCE

MAINS

19 — PAPRIKA AUBERGINE SALAD

20 — SALMON AND RICE STEW

21 — ROSEMARY MUSHROOM AND CARROT STEW

22 — BBQ BEEF

23 — LAMB AND TOMATOES

24 — PAPRIKA CHICKEN BAKE

MEAT

25 BEEF AND CARROTS

26 BEEF AND PEACH SAUCE

27 SAUSAGE STEW

28 LAMB AND BEANS

29 ITALIAN BEEF

30 LAMB AND ENDIVES

SIDES

31 BUTTERY ARTICHOKES

32 MINTY SPINACH SAUTÉ

33 PARMESAN BRUSSELS SPROUTS

34 BALSAMIC RED CABBAGE

35 CINNAMON SQUASH

36 OKRA MIX

VEGETABLES

37 CREAMY OKRA

38 CHILLI ARTICHOKES

39 FENNEL AND PARMESAN

40 GARLIC FENNEL

41 CABBAGE BAKE

42 GINGER BOK CHOY

STARTERS

43 BEETROOT DIP

44 TOMATOES AND MUSHROOMS SALSA

45 SQUASH AND COURGETTE DIP

46 BROCCOLI AND CARROTS SPREAD

47 APPLE DIP

48 SWEET POTATO DIP

DESSERTS

49 BANANA CAKE

50 PEARS STEW

51 COCOA BARS

52 MAPLE PEAR PUDDING

53 CARAMELIZED FIGS

54 GUAVA CAKE

BREAKFAST

Homemade British Cooking Chapter: 1

CHERRIES OATS

BREAKFAST RECIPE

Ingredients

- 700ml of almond milk
- 135g of rolled oats
- 60g of pitted and chopped cherries
- Four whisked eggs
- 60g of cream cheese
- A tbsp of Light brown sugar
- 1g of cinnamon powder

Directions

1. In a bowl, mix all the mentioned ingredients and toss well.
2. Pour the combination into your Ninja Foodi Smartlid, close the pressure lid and cook the mixture on High for fifteen minutes.
3. Release pressure naturally for ten mins, divide the oats into bowls and serve.

Cooking & Prep Time: 20

Servings: 4

MUSHROOM AND SPINACH BAKE

BREAKFAST RECIPE

Ingredients

- Eight sliced brown mushrooms
- 25g of torn spinach
- Four whisked eggs
- Eight halved cherry tomatoes
- Two tbsp of chopped spring onions
- 15ml of extra virgin essential olive oil
- Salt and black pepper

Directions

1. Set the Foodi Smartlid on Sauté mode, add the oil, heat it up, add the onions along with the mushrooms, stir and cook for 5 minutes.
2. Add the rest of the components, toss, set the machine on Bake mode and cook at 180ºC for fifteen mins.
3. Transfer to platters and serve.

Cooking & Prep Time: 30

Servings: 4

ALMOND EGGS

BREAKFAST RECIPE

Ingredients

- 90ml of almond milk
- A drizzle of Worcestershire sauce
- 60g of grated cheddar cheese
- Four whisked eggs
- A chopped red onion.
- 15ml of extra virgin olive oil

Directions

1. Select the Sauté cooking function on your Ninja Foodi Smartlid, pour the oil, heat it, add the onion, stir and cook for 5 minutes.
2. In a bowl, mix all the other components and whisk well.
3. Add the mix to the onion, toss, set the Foodi on Bake mode and cook at 190ºC for ten mins. Transfer to platters and serve.

Cooking & Prep Time: 20

Servings: 4

SMOKED SAUSAGE BREAKFAST MIX

BREAKFAST RECIPE

Ingredients

- 680g of browned and sliced smoked sausage
- 460g of shredded cheddar cheese
- Four whisked eggs
- 1g of garlic powder
- A tsp and half of chopped thyme
- A pinch of salt & black pepper
- Cooking spray

Directions

1. Place the reversible rack within the Foodi, add the baking pan inside and grease it with cooking spray.
2. Mix all the listed components except the cheese and toss them into the pan.
3. Add the cheese on the top, set the device on Baking mode and cook at 180°C for thirty mins.
4. Transfer to serving platters and serve.

Cooking & Prep Time: 40

Servings: 4

CREAM CHEESE AND BREAD BOWLS

BREAKFAST RECIPE

Ingredients

- 100g of cubed bread loaf
- 220g of cubed cream cheese
- 500g of heavy cream
- 110g of Light brown sugar
- Four of eggs
- A tsp of cinnamon powder
- A tsp of vanilla flavour
- Cooking spray

Directions

1. Grease your Foodi with the cooking spray, add all the listed components and toss.
2. Set the Ninja Foodi on Air Crisp and cook for a quarter-hour. Divide into bowls and serve.

Cooking & Prep Time: 25

Servings: 6

YOGURT HASH BROWNS

BREAKFAST RECIPE

Ingredients

- 680g of hash browns
- 120g of Greek yoghurt
- A tbsp of chopped chives
- 30ml of rapeseed oil
- Salt and black pepper

Directions

1. Mix all the listed components inside your Ninja Foodi Smartlid Max except for the yoghurt, set the unit on the Air Crisp cooking mode and cook for fifteen mins.
2. Add the yoghurt, toss, transfer to serving into bowls and serve.

Cooking & Prep Time: 20

Servings: 4

FISH & SEAFOOD

Homemade British Cooking   Chapter: 2

SEA BASS FILLETS

SEAFOOD RECIPE

Ingredients

- Four boneless medium sea bass fillets
- Eight minced garlic cloves
- 80ml of essential olive oil
- A tbsp of grated lemon zest
- A tbsp of freshly squeezed lemon juice
- Salt and black pepper

Directions

1. Put the reversible rack in the Ninja Foodi Max, add the baking pan inside and mix all the listed components inside.
2. Set your Ninja Foodi on Baking mode and cook this mixture at 190°C for twenty-five mins.
3. Transfer to serving platters and serve.

Cooking & Prep Time: 30

Servings: 4

ROSEMARY SHRIMP

SEAFOOD RECIPE

Ingredients

- 450g of peeled and deveined shrimp
- A tbsp of chopped rosemary
- 30ml of essential olive oil
- Salt and black pepper

Directions

1. In a bowl, mix all the listed ingredients and toss.
2. Put the Foodi's basket into the unit and place the shrimp within it.
3. Cook on Air Crisp at 180°C for ten mins, divide between plates and serve.

Cooking & Prep Time: 13

Servings: 4

TUNA AND SPINACH

SEAFOOD RECIPE

Ingredients

- 450g skinless, boneless and cubed tuna
- 30g of melted butter
- 60g torn spinach
- Salt and black pepper

Directions

1. In your Foodi, mix all the ingredients, close the pressure lid and cook on High for 12 minutes.
2. Release the pressure quickly for 5 minutes, divide everything between plates and serve.

Cooking & Prep Time: 17

Servings: 4

PARMESAN SHRIMP

SEAFOOD RECIPE

Ingredients

- 450g of peeled and deveined shrimp
- 60g of grated parmesan
- Three minced garlic cloves
- 60g of soft butter
- A tsp of dried oregano

Directions

1. In your Foodi, mix all the listed ingredients except the parmesan, close the pressure lid and cook on High for ten minutes.
2. Release the pressure quickly for 4 minutes, transfer to serving bowls, sprinkle the parmesan over and serve.

Cooking & Prep Time: 14

Servings: 4

SALMON AND SPRING ONIONS

SEAFOOD RECIPE

Ingredients

- Four boneless salmon fillets
- Four chopped spring onions
- 15g of melted butter
- Juice of one lemon
- Salt and black pepper

Directions

1. Put the reversible rack inside the Ninja Foodi Max Smartlid, add the baking pan inside and mix all the mentioned ingredients inside the pan.
2. Cook on Baking mode at 195ºC for 20 minutes, divide between plates and serve.

Cooking & Prep Time: 30

Servings: 4

MISO SALMON

SEAFOOD RECIPE

Ingredients

- 450g of boneless, skinless and cubed salmon fillets
- A chopped sweet onion
- Two minced garlic cloves
- A quarter cup of miso
- 15ml of rice vinegar
- 5g of sugar
- 5g of mustard

Directions

1. In your Foodi Max, mix all the ingredients, close the pressure lid and cook on High for 12 minutes.
2. Release pressure quickly for 5 minutes, divide a mixture into bowls and serve.

Cooking & Prep Time: 17

Servings: 4

POULTRY

Homemade British Cooking   Chapter: 3

CHICKEN AND ONION SAUCE

POULTRY RECIPE

Ingredients

- 680g of boneless, skinless and cubed chicken breasts
- 160g of chopped yellow onion
- 250ml of chicken stock
- 15ml of essential olive oil
- Two tsp of sweet paprika
- Salt and black pepper

Directions

1. Set the Foodi on Sauté mode, add the oil, and heat it, add the onions and sauté for ten mins.
2. Add all the other ingredients, close the pressure lid on and cook on High for fifteen minutes.
3. Release the pressure naturally for ten mins, divide everything between plates and serve.

Cooking & Prep Time: 35

Servings: 6

CHICKEN MEATBALLS

POULTRY RECIPE

Ingredients

- 450g of ground chicken meat
- A whisked egg
- Four minced garlic cloves
- A minced yellow onion
- 60g of bread crumbs
- 200g of Single cream
- 15g of chopped parsley
- 30ml of organic extra virgin olive oil
- 30g of butter
- Salt and black pepper

Directions

1. In a bowl, combine all the listed components except the oil, butter and single cream, stir and shape small meatballs out of the mixture.
2. Select the Sauté cooking function in your Ninja Foodi Smartlid, add the oil and butter, heat it up, and add the meatballs and brown for 5 minutes.
3. Add the single cream, close the pressure lid and cook on High for 15 mins.
4. Release pressure fast for 5 minutes, divide between plates and serve.

Cooking & Prep Time: 25

Servings: 4

PAPRIKA TURKEY

POULTRY RECIPE

Ingredients

- Two kinless, boneless turkey breasts
- 250ml of chicken stock
- A chopped yellow onion
- 45g of melted butter
- A tsp of sweet paprika
- Salt and black pepper

Directions

1. Set the Foodi Smartlid on Sauté mode, add the butter, heat it, and add the onion and sauté for 2 minutes.
2. Add the turkey and brown for two more minutes.
3. Add the others ingredients, seal the pressure lid and cook on High for 16 minutes.
4. Release the pressure naturally for 10 minutes, divide between plates and serve.

Cooking & Prep Time: 30

Servings: 4

DUCK AND LENTILS

POULTRY RECIPE

Ingredients

- 450 to 900g of duck, cut into pieces
- 120ml of chicken stock
- 250g of drained canned lentils
- 60g of tomato sauce
- Two chopped red onions
- Four minced garlic cloves
- 15ml of essential organic olive oil
- Salt and black pepper

Directions

1. Select the Sauté cooking function on your Ninja Foodi, add the oil, heat it, add the duck pieces, stir and brown them for five mins.
2. Add the rest of the listed components, seal the pressure lid and cook on High for twenty-five.
3. Release the pressure quickly for five mins, transfer to platters and serve.

Cooking & Prep Time: 35

Servings: 4

CHICKEN AND COURGETTE

POULTRY RECIPE

Ingredients

- 450g of skinless and boneless chicken breasts
- Two roughly cubed courgettes
- A chopped yellow onion
- Three minced garlic cloves
- 30ml of essential extra virgin olive oil
- Juice of one lime
- Salt and black pepper

Directions

1. In your Foodi, combine all the mentioned ingredients, close the pressure lid and cook on High for 25 minutes.
2. Use the natural method to release the pressure for ten mins, transfer to platters and serve.

Cooking & Prep Time: 30

Servings: 4

CHICKEN AND CHILIES SAUCE

POULTRY RECIPE

Ingredients

- 450g of skinless, boneless and cubed chicken breasts
- 200g chopped tomatoes
- Six chopped canned green chillies
- A chopped yellow onion
- A minced garlic clove
- 30ml of extra virgin olive oil
- Salt and black pepper

Directions

1. Select the Sauté cooking function on your Ninja Foodi, add the oil, and heat up.
2. Then add chillies, tomatoes, garlic, onions salt and pepper, stir and sauté for ten mins.
3. Add the chicken, seal the pressure lid and cook on High for fifteen mins.
4. Release the pressure naturally for ten mins, transfer to platters and serve.

Cooking & Prep Time: 35

Servings: 4

MAINS

Homemade British Cooking — Chapter: 4

PAPRIKA AUBERGINE SALAD

MAIN RECIPE

Ingredients

- Four cubed Aubergines
- Juice of one lime
- Three minced garlic cloves
- 120g of tomato sauce
- 15ml of organic extra virgin olive oil
- Two tsp of sweet paprika
- Salt and black pepper

Directions

1. Set the Ninja Foodi Smartlid on Sauté mode, add the oil, heat it, add the garlic, stir and cook for 1 minute.
2. Add the rest of the ingredients, toss, close the pressure lid and cook on High for 15 minutes.
3. Release the pressure quickly for 5 minutes, divide this mixture into bowls and serve.

Cooking & Prep Time: 20

Servings: 4

SALMON AND RICE STEW

MAIN RECIPE

Ingredients

- 680g of salmon fillet
- 400ml of veggie stock
- 140g wild rice
- A chopped red pepper
- A chopped yellow onion
- 15ml of essential extra virgin olive oil
- Salt and black pepper

Directions

1. Set the Foodi Max on Sauté mode, add the oil, heat it, add the onion and pepper, stir and sauté for 5 minutes.
2. Add other ingredients, toss, close the pressure lid and cook on High for twenty minutes.
3. Release pressure naturally for 10 minutes, divide the stew into bowls and serve.

Cooking & Prep Time: 35

Servings: 4

ROSEMARY MUSHROOM AND CARROT STEW

MAIN RECIPE

Ingredients

- 450g of sliced white mushrooms
- 60g of tomato sauce
- 30g of torn spinach
- Two sliced carrots
- A chopped yellow onion
- 15ml of essential organic olive oil
- 0.5g of chopped rosemary

Directions

1. Set your Ninja Foodi Smartlid on Sauté mode add the oil, heat it, add the mushrooms and also the onion, stir and sauté for 5 minutes.
2. Add other ingredients, toss, position pressure lid on, cook on High for 15 minutes, and release pressure naturally for ten mins.
3. Divide the stew into bowls and serve.

Cooking & Prep Time: 30

Servings: 4

BBQ BEEF

MAIN RECIPE

Ingredients

- 450g of cubed beef stew meat
- A sliced red pepper
- A cup of bbq sauce
- A sliced green pepper
- 15ml of essential extra virgin olive oil
- A tsp of chopped rosemary
- Salt and black pepper

Directions

1. Set the Foodi on Sauté mode, add the oil, heat it, add the meat, rosemary, salt & pepper, toss and brown for three to four mins.
2. Add all the other ingredients, toss, close the pressure lid and cook on High for 25 minutes.
3. Release the pressure naturally for ten mins, transfer to bowls and serve.

Cooking & Prep Time: 55

Servings: 4

LAMB AND TOMATOES

MAIN RECIPE

Ingredients

- 450g of cubed lamb stew meat
- 250g of chopped cherry tomatoes
- 15ml of organic olive oil
- 15ml of balsamic vinegar
- A tbsp of chopped rosemary
- 30g of grated parmesan

Directions

1. Set the Foodi on Sauté mode, add the oil, and heat it.
2. Add the lamb and brown for three to four mins.
3. Add the rest of the components except for the parmesan, close the pressure lid and cook on High for 25 minutes.
4. Release pressure naturally for ten mins, divide between plates, add the parmesan over and serve.

Cooking & Prep Time: 40

Servings: 4

PAPRIKA CHICKEN BAKE

MAIN RECIPE

Ingredients

- Two skinless, boneless and cubed chicken breasts
- 240g of tomato sauce
- 15ml of essential olive oil
- Two tsp of sweet paprika
- Salt and black pepper

Directions

1. Set the Foodi on Sauté mode, add the oil, and heat it, add the chicken and brown for five mins.
2. Add the rest of the components, toss, set your Ninja Foodi on Baking mode and cook at 190°C for 20 mins.
3. Divide between plates and serve.

Cooking & Prep Time: 35

Servings: 4

MEAT

Homemade British Cooking · Chapter: 5

BEEF AND CARROTS

MEAT RECIPE

Ingredients

- 450g of cubed beef stew meat
- 250ml beef stock
- A chopped yellow onion
- Two minced garlic cloves
- Three sliced carrots
- 15ml of organic extra virgin olive oil
- Salt and black pepper

Directions

1. Set the Ninja Foodi Smartlid on Sauté mode, add the oil, and heat it.
2. Add the onion and garlic and sauté for five mins.
3. Add the beef with the rest of the ingredients, close the pressure lid and cook on High for 25 minutes.
4. Release pressure naturally for ten mins, divide the mixture between plates and serve.

Cooking & Prep Time: 40

Servings: 4

BEEF AND PEACH SAUCE

MEAT RECIPE

Ingredients

- 450g of cubed beef stew meat
- A chopped red onion
- A minced garlic oil
- 60g of peach preserves
- 30ml of essential organic olive oil

Directions

1. Set the Foodi Smartlid on Sauté mode, add the oil, and heat it.
2. Add the onion and the garlic and sauté for four mins.
3. Add the rest of the ingredients, close the pressure lid and cook on High for 25 minutes.
4. Release pressure naturally for ten mins, divide into bowls and serve.

Cooking & Prep Time: 35

Servings: 4

SAUSAGE STEW

MEAT RECIPE

Ingredients

- Four sliced sausage links
- 280g of crushed canned tomatoes
- A chopped red onion
- 15ml of essential olive oil
- A tbsp of sweet paprika
- Salt and black pepper

Directions

1. Set the Foodi Max on Sauté mode, add the oil, and heat it, add the onion and sausages and brown them for five mins.
2. Add other ingredients, close the pressure lid and cook on High for 15 mins.
3. Release pressure quickly for 5 minutes, divide everything into bowls and serve.

Cooking & Prep Time: 25

Servings: 4

LAMB AND BEANS

MEAT RECIPE

Ingredients

- 680g of cubed lamb stew meat
- Two cups of drained and rinsed canned black beans
- 240g of tomato sauce
- Two minced garlic cloves
- 30ml of organic olive oil
- Salt and black pepper

Directions

1. Set the Foodi on Sauté mode, add the oil, heat it, add the meat, and garlic and brown them for five mins.
2. Add the rest of the ingredients, close the pressure lid and cook on High for twenty minutes.
3. Release pressure naturally for ten mins, divide the mixture between plates and serve.

Cooking & Prep Time: 35

Servings: 4

ITALIAN BEEF

MEAT RECIPE

Ingredients

- 900g of cubed beef stew meat
- Six cubed tomatoes
- Three chopped garlic cloves
- 30ml of essential olive oil
- A tsp of dried thyme
- A tsp dried basil
- 500ml of Pomegranate Juice
- Salt and black pepper

Directions

1. Set the Foodi Smartlid on Sauté mode, add the oil, heat it, add the beef and garlic, stir and brown for five mins
2. Add the other ingredients, close the stress lid and cook on High for 20 minutes.
3. Release pressure naturally for 10 mins, divide into bowls and serve.

Cooking & Prep Time: 35

Servings: 6

LAMB AND ENDIVES

MEAT RECIPE

Ingredients

- Four Lamb chops
- 120ml of beef stock
- Four shredded endives
- 30ml of essential olive oil
- A tbsp of chopped rosemary
- Salt and black pepper

Directions

1. In your Ninja Foodi Smartlid, mix all the listed components, close the pressure lid and cook on High for 25 minutes.
2. Release the pressure quickly for 5 minutes, divide everything between plates and serve.

Cooking & Prep Time: 30

Servings: 4

SIDES

Homemade British Cooking   Chapter: 6

BUTTERY ARTICHOKES

SIDE RECIPE

Ingredients

- Four trimmed artichokes; cut into quarters
- Three minced garlic cloves
- 45g of melted butter

Directions

1. Put the reversible rack inside the Smartlid Ninja Foodi, add the baking pan inside and mix all the ingredients into it.
2. Set your machine on Baking mode, cook at 190°C for 20 mins, divide between plates and serve.

Cooking & Prep Time: 25

Servings: 4

MINTY SPINACH SAUTÉ

SIDE RECIPE

Ingredients

- 450g torn spinach leaves
- 15g chopped green onions
- 7g chopped mint leaves
- 15ml of balsamic vinegar
- 5ml of extra virgin olive oil
- 5ml of lime juice
- Salt and black pepper

Directions

1. Set the Foodi on Sauté mode, add the oil, heat it down, add the onions, stir and cook for just two minutes.
2. Add the other ingredients, toss, close the pressure lid and cook on High for 5 minutes.
3. Release the pressure fast for 5 minutes, divide between plates and serve.

Cooking & Prep Time: 12

Servings: 4

PARMESAN BRUSSELS SPROUTS

SIDE RECIPE

Ingredients

- 900g halved Brussels sprouts
- 15ml of organic olive oil
- 60g of grated parmesan
- Salt and black pepper

Directions

1. Combine all the mentioned components into the basket of your Ninja Foodi Max Smartlid except the cheese, toss and set the unit on Air Crisp cooking mode and cook at 185°C for twenty minutes.
2. Transfer to serving platters, add the cheese over and serve.

Cooking & Prep Time: 25

Servings: 4

BALSAMIC RED CABBAGE

SIDE RECIPE

Ingredients

- A shredded red cabbage head
- Four minced garlic cloves
- 15ml of balsamic vinegar
- 15ml of extra virgin essential olive oil
- Salt and black pepper

Directions

1. Select the Sauté cooking function on your Ninja Foodi Max Smartlid, add the oil, heat it, add the garlic, stir and cook for around two to three mins.
2. Add the rest of the components, seal the lid and cook on High pressure for twelve mins.
3. Release the pressure naturally for ten mins, transfer to serving platters and serve.

Cooking & Prep Time: 25

Servings: 4

CINNAMON SQUASH

SIDE RECIPE

Ingredients

- A peeled and cubed butternut squash
- Two minced garlic cloves
- A julienned red onion
- 60ml of veggie stock
- A half tsp of cinnamon powder
- A half tsp of grated ginger
- Cooking spray

Directions

1. Put the reversible rack inside Foodi, add the baking pan inside and grease it with cooking spray.
2. Add the remaining components inside, toss, select the Baking cooking function on your Ninja Foodi Smartlid and cook at 180°C for twenty-five mins.
3. Transfer the mixture to bolws and serve.

Cooking & Prep Time: 25

Servings: 4

OKRA MIX

SIDE RECIPE

Ingredients

- 450g of halved okra
- 250ml of veggie stock
- Two chopped spring onions
- A tsp of minced garlic
- 5ml of essential extra virgin olive oil
- A tbsp of chopped coriander
- Salt and black pepper

Directions

1. Put the reversible rack inside your Ninja Foodi Smartlid, add the baking pan inside and mix the ingredients into it.
2. Select the Baking cooking function on your Ninja Foodi and cook at 195ºC for twenty mins.
3. Transfer to serving platters and serve.

Cooking & Prep Time: 30

Servings: 6

VEGETABLES

Homemade British Cooking

Chapter: 7

CREAMY OKRA

VEGGIE RECIPE

Ingredients

- 450g of okra
- Six minced garlic cloves
- 250ml of buttermilk
- A drizzle of organic olive oil
- Salt and black pepper

Directions

1. Select the Sauté cooking function on your Ninja Foodi, add the oil, heat it up, add the garlic and cook for around two mins.
2. Add the remaining mentioned components, close the pressure lid on and cook on High for ten mins.
3. Release pressure quickly for five mins, transfer to serving bowls and serve.

Cooking & Prep Time: 17

Servings: 4

CHILLI ARTICHOKES

VEGGIE RECIPE

Ingredients

- Two trimmed and halved big artichokes
- 30ml of organic essential olive oil
- Two tsp of chilli powder
- Juice of one lemon
- Salt and black pepper

Directions

1. Combine all the mentioned components into the basket of your Ninja Foodi Smartlid, toss and cook on Air Crisp at 200°C for 15 minutes.
2. Transfer the artichokes to serving platters and serve.

Cooking & Prep Time: 20

Servings: 4

FENNEL AND PARMESAN

VEGGIE RECIPE

Ingredients

- Two sliced big fennel bulbs
- A sliced red onion
- 30g of grated parmesan
- 15ml of balsamic vinegar
- 15ml of essential olive oil
- A pinch of salt and black pepper

Directions

1. Combine all the mentioned components into the basket of your Ninja Foodi Smartlid except the cheese, close the pressure lid and cook on High for eight mins.
2. Release the pressure quickly for five mins, Transfer to serving platters, add the cheese on top and serve.

Cooking & Prep Time: 13

Servings: 4

GARLIC FENNEL

VEGGIE RECIPE

Ingredients

- Two fennel bulbs; cut into wedges
- 30g of pomegranate seeds
- 60ml of orange juice
- 120ml of chicken stock
- Two minced garlic cloves
- 30ml of olive oil
- 30ml of pomegranate juice
- Salt and black pepper

Directions

1. In your Foodi; combine all the ingredients, close the pressure lid and cook on High for eight mins.
2. Release the pressure quickly for five mins, divide between bowls and serve.

Cooking & Prep Time: 13

Servings: 4

CABBAGE BAKE

VEGGIE RECIPE

Ingredients

- 560g of crushed canned tomatoes
- Four cups of shredded red cabbage
- 60ml of chicken stock
- A pinch of salt and black pepper
- Cooking spray
- 30g of raisins
- Grated zest of one lemon

Directions

1. Put the reversible rack from the Foodi, add the baking pan inside and grease it with cooking spray.
2. Mix all the mentioned components in the pan and cook in Baking mode at 195°C for twenty mins.
3. Transfer the mixture to serving platters and serve.

Cooking & Prep Time: 25

Servings: 4

GINGER BOK CHOY

VEGGIE RECIPE

Ingredients

- 450g torn bok choy
- 30ml of essential olive oil
- 30ml of lemon juice
- Two tsp of grated ginger
- Salt and black pepper

Directions

1. Select the Sauté cooking function on your Ninja Foodi Max Smartlid, add the oil, heat it, add the ginger and cook for about one minute.
2. Add the other ingredients, close the pressure lid and cook on High for around nine mins.
3. Release the pressure quickly for five mins, transfer the bok choy to plates and serve.

Cooking & Prep Time: 15

Servings: 4

STARTERS

Homemade British Cooking Chapter: 8

BEETROOT DIP

STARTER RECIPE

Ingredients

- Eight chopped beetroots
- Eight minced garlic cloves
- 250ml of veggie stock
- 60ml of fresh lemon juice
- A chopped yellow onion
- 30ml of extra virgin organic olive oil
- Salt and black pepper

Directions

1. Select the Sauté cooking function on your Ninja Foodi Max Smartlid, add the oil, heat up, and add the onion with the garlic, stir and cook for around four mins.
2. Add all the remaining components, close the pressure lid and cook on High for twenty mins.
3. Release the pressure naturally for ten min and blend the mixture using an immersion blender.
4. Transfer to serving bowls and serve.

Cooking & Prep Time: 35

Servings: 6

TOMATOES AND MUSHROOMS SALSA

STARTER RECIPE

Ingredients

- 450g of sliced shiitake mushrooms
- Eight cherry tomatoes; cut into quarters
- A chopped yellow onion
- Three minced garlic cloves
- 60g of coconut cream
- A tbsp of minced coriander
- 15ml of organic olive oil
- Salt and black pepper

Directions

1. Select the Sauté cooking function on your Ninja Foodi Max Smartlid, add the oil, heat up, add the onion and also the garlic and cook for about five mins.
2. Add the other ingredients, close the pressure lid and cook on High for twenty mins.
3. Release the pressure naturally for ten mins, divide the salsa between bowls and serve.

Cooking & Prep Time: 35

Servings: 6

SQUASH AND COURGETTE DIP

STARTER RECIPE

Ingredients

- 900g of peeled and cubed butternut squash
- A chopped yellow onion
- A chopped courgette
- 250ml of veggie stock
- 15ml of essential organic olive oil
- Salt and black pepper

Directions

1. Select the Sauté cooking function on your Ninja Foodi, add the oil, and heat up, add the onion and sauté for around three mins.
2. Add all the other ingredients, close the pressure lid and cook on High for fifteen mins.
3. Release the pressure naturally for ten min and blend the mixture using an immersion blender.
4. Transfer the dip to serving bowls and serve.

Cooking & Prep Time: 30

Servings: 8

BROCCOLI AND CARROTS SPREAD

STARTER RECIPE

Ingredients

- Eight minced garlic cloves
- 420g of broccoli florets
- 500ml of veggie stock
- Four sliced carrots
- 30g of melted butter
- Salt and black pepper

Directions

1. In your Foodi mix all the ingredients, close the pressure lid and cook on High for twenty mins.
2. Release the pressure naturally for ten mins, blend this mixture using an immersion blender, divide it into bowls and serve as a spread.

Cooking & Prep Time: 30

Servings: 6

APPLE DIP

STARTER RECIPE

Ingredients

- Eight cored and chopped apples
- 120ml of water
- A tsp of cinnamon powder

Directions

1. In your Foodi, combine all the ingredients, close the pressure lid and cook on High for fifteen mins.
2. Release pressure naturally for ten mins, blend this apple mix using an immersion blender, transfer the mixture to bowls and serve it cold.

Cooking & Prep Time: 25

Servings: 4

SWEET POTATO DIP

STARTER RECIPE

Ingredients

- 750g of crushed canned tomatoes
- 300g chopped sweet potato
- Three minced garlic cloves
- Salt and black pepper

Directions

1. In your Foodi Smartlid, combine all the listed components, close the pressure lid and cook on High for twenty mins.
2. Release the pressure naturally for ten mins, use an immersion blender to blend this mixture and then transfer into bowls and serve.

Cooking & Prep Time: 30

Servings: 6

DESSERTS

Homemade British Cooking · Chapter: 9

BANANA CAKE

DESSERT RECIPE

Ingredients

- Three peeled and mashed bananas
- Two whisked eggs
- 250ml of buttermilk
- 70g of white sugar
- 180g of white flour
- 30ml of freshly squeezed lemon juice
- 30ml of rapeseed oil
- A tsp of baking powder
- A tsp of vanilla extract
- Cooking spray

Directions

1. Combine all the listed ingredients except the cooking spray in a bowl and whisk.
2. Put the reversible rack into your Ninja Foodi Smartlid, add the cake pan inside, grease it with cooking spray and pour the cake mixture inside it.
3. Set your machine on Baking mode, cook the dessert at 175°C for 35 minutes, slice and serve cold.

Cooking & Prep Time: 40

Servings: 10

PEARS STEW

DESSERT RECIPE

Ingredients

- Four peeled and halved pears
- 100g of sugar
- 250ml of orange juice

Directions

1. Mix the ingredients you have on the list in your Ninja Foodi Smartlid, close the pressure lid, and cook on High for 15 mins.
2. Release the pressure fast for five mins, divide into bowls and serve.

Cooking & Prep Time: 20

Servings: 4

COCOA BARS

DESSERT RECIPE

Ingredients

- 80g of chopped chocolate
- 240g of melted butter
- 120g of white flour
- 300g of sugar
- Four whisked eggs
- A tsp of vanilla flavouring
- A tbsp of powdered cocoa
- Cooking spray

Directions

1. In a bowl, combine all the ingredients except the cooking spray and whisk.
2. Put the reversible rack inside your Ninja Foodi Smartlid, add the wedding cake pan inside, grease it with cooking spray and pour the cocoa mix inside.
3. Select the Baking cooking function on the Ninja Foodi and cook at 175°C for twenty-five mins.
4. Cut into bars and serve cold.

Cooking & Prep Time: 35

Servings: 8

MAPLE PEAR PUDDING

DESSERT RECIPE

Ingredients

- Two peeled and chopped big pears
- 240ml almond milk
- 250of maple syrup
- Two whisked eggs
- A tbsp of Cornflour

Directions

1. In a bowl, combine all the mentioned components, whisk and transfer to a ramekin.
2. Put the reversible rack inside the Ninja Foodi Max Smartlid, place ramekin inside, cook on Baking mode at 170ºC for twenty-five mins, divide between cups and serve cold.

Cooking & Prep Time: 35

Servings: 4

CARAMELIZED FIGS

DESSERT RECIPE

Ingredients

- Eight halved figs
- 10g of honey
- Cooking spray
- A tsp of sugar

Directions

1. In a bowl, mix the figs with the remainder of the ingredients and toss.
2. Put the figs together with your Smartlid Foodi's basket and cook on Air Crisp at 175°C for ten mins. Serve warm.

Cooking & Prep Time: 15

Servings: 4

GUAVA CAKE

DESSERT RECIPE

Ingredients

- Two peeled and flesh-chopped guavas
- 200g of sugar
- 60g of butter
- Four whisked eggs
- 120g of white flour
- A tsp of baking powder
- Cooking spray

Directions

1. Combine all the listed components except the cooking spray in a bowl and stir.
2. Put the reversible rack in the Ninja Foodi Smartlid, place the cake pan inside, grease it with cooking spray and pour the wedding cake mixture inside.
3. Set the Ninja Foodi on Baking mode and cook at 175°C for twenty-five mins.
4. Leave the cake to rest before you slice and serve it.

Cooking & Prep Time: 30

Servings: 4

Printed in Great Britain
by Amazon

10914325R00045